With special appreciation to my teacher

LURDES SARAMAGO CHAPPELL

author of

The Branches of the Trees Cover Us All

IN A LANGUAGE NOT YOUR OWN

Poems in English Shaped by an English–Portuguese Dialogue

SONJA N. BOHM

Published by Sonja N. Bohm

ISBN: 979-8-9995-7092-5

In a Language Not Your Own: Poems in English Shaped by an English–Portuguese Dialogue

First Edition

O verso não é bom, mas não me ocorre
Nenhum outro melhor neste momento.

The verse is not good, but no better one
comes to mind at the moment.

—Bulhão Pato, *Paquita* (Canto I)

AT THE EDGE OF THE STREET

Speak to me in a language
not your own.
Hold me in the moonlight
at the edge of the street,
without a care
for the man at the window.
Promise me the sun,
not another farewell.

Contents

Between Bank and Boat

Those who sing in summer hope to see the sea.

—Eugénio de Andrade

SEPTEMBER

Will it always be September?—
the month of unspeakable longing?
That space between bank and boat,
the vast and impassable moat,
says yes.

But the birds sing—
they sing from birth,
and discover they have wings.
Across that divide, they fly.
They say no—

September will not last,
only what is in the heart.
So that which only seems
gives way to dreams,
and says, "Perhaps!"

I CAME AS A STRANGER

I came as a stranger,
even as a friend;
but I sang like a lover
and fell in love with you.

"COLD FEET"

Can I know this country
without putting my feet in the waters?
I hear these waters are cold.
I am accustomed to the cold;
my feet often get cold,
but hardly ever wet!

ONLY A PROFILE

The mouth of the river,
 the receding waves,
 the coastal garden…
This profile is all that I see;
the rest is hidden—
 beneath the waters,
 below the earth…
But it was never mine to take;
it was always yours to give.

BODIES OF WATER

The oceans are continuous and
interconnected bodies of water.
They are waters without limits,
except for those defined by humans.
And we are like these waters:
bodies separated only by convention,
if not by God.

EVERYTHING

When I am near the waters,
they are all that I see;
when I am away from the waters,
I see them in everything.

UNCONDITIONAL

When I gaze upon the sea,
it returns my gaze to me,
reflecting the state of my soul.

When I turn away to depart,
it refuses to judge my heart,
and asks nothing of me at all.

INDIFFERENT

The waters are indifferent
to my desire to be near.
They assume no responsibility
for my doubt and fear.
Still, their presence
is a source of comfort
even though they are, at the same time,
a source of my unrest.

NAZARÉ ("ET VIVAM")

I dive into the waters of your eyes.
In them I swim without hesitation,
for you accept me without judgment.

Your mercy defies description.
The ebb and flow of the tides
is a balm for my heart.

I stand upon the cliffs of Nazaré,
wavering between intensity and serenity;
but I accept this duality in good faith,

knowing that stability is born from their union.
Therefore, I do not fear life's highs and lows,
for I am able to navigate any storm.

WHITE SAILS

In waves they return:

White sails that pass

through my mind and memory;

some days with clarity,

and other days

through tears…

Neither good nor bad,

just days in degrees.

I wait on the shore for a boat.

THE DISTANCE

I choose to not live a life at sea;
but even though my feet are on land,
I look toward the waters like a sailor
who searches the horizon for his homeland.
They see it in my eyes: the Distance.
I am absent in my dreams, adrift...

FROM BOW TO STERN

From bow to stern,
 from starboard to port,
heavy-laden
he suffers the weight.

Wave upon wave,
captured by the swell,
his hull flexes
with deep groaning.

FATE

Fate waits near the sea
  and counts the boats, the birds…
But it will not fly, nor will it sail;
it moves only when the winds blow.

RECKLESS WATERS

Reckless waters surge
headlong between fragrant banks
hungry for the sea.

REFUGE

When is it that I will see you?
    Who is it that can tell me?
Will I see you one more time?
    Five times? Maybe ten?

If I never do return,
    it will not have been in vain.
For I've gazed upon the sea;
    it was my salvation.

I TURNED MY BACK

I turned my back on the waters—
what else could I do?
I turned my back on the waters
because I could not stay.
I turned my back on the waters,
but this I can say:—
I'll come back to the waters
because I'm not done singing.

THE SEAGULLS

The seagulls sing here too;—
just as there, they sing.
And like there, they come and go—
here also, returning...
But here is not there, I know!—
Still, I will sing;
and like the birds, I will return—
I will always return from the sea.

NOT NOW

Not now.

Not now, but some day.

Some day I'll return.

I'll return in this boat.

In this boat, to these shores...

To these shores in this boat

I'll return some day.

Some day, but not now.

Not now.

Rumors of April

What can a man expect when,

so childishly,

he exposes himself thus to the sun, in living flesh?

—Eugénio de Andrade

AUTUMN

Thinking not of the cold,
we'll bring forth the winter;
till we live with nothing,
we haven't lived life!

Child of September, I'm waiting...
Chill of autumn, come with haste!

WINTER

Here it comes again: the emptiness—
the restlessness not meant for an eternal being.
But I'll not force the days to rhyme
like a trite poem with sounds
that return upon themselves—
that please the ears,
yet numb the soul—no!
I will sleep, but I will dream,
and awake renewed.

RUMORS OF APRIL

So immense, this nothingness!—
The whiteness of the page, how blinding!
Even the word on the street
lacks substance—
tame, the gossip of the people
that once bared its teeth.
Stagnant, the currents
that once flowed from the pen: now
without direction, but not without hope;
for the winds will return,
blown from their source,
to inspire us anew!

A HAPPY FACE

If only this emptiness
was for things of this earth:—
the temporal, the ephemeral, the physical...
But I'll drink from this cup
with a happy face,
and hope that I suffer alone.

FAITHLESS IS THE HAND

Faithless is the hand
 that writes in desperation
and wears out the pen.

FRAGMENT

By the light of the gibbous moon, I walked alone.
It was December, just before the Cold Moon.

******

Paralyzed by a fear
that surpasses my desire,
I longed for release...
Of what value is loyalty
without love in the heart?

To deny myself
the things I most desire
is to suspend the breath
and stop the heart;—
I will extinguish like flames without oxygen.

But who am I?
What right have I to these waters,

these stones, the moonlight?
Whose dream is it
that I'm dreaming?

And where am I now?
Where is the compass that used to
fit so well in the hand?—
the time spent on nothing
but your attention?

The shadows speak—

"Come, let us play like children.
We will sing like songbirds
and dance on our graves."

and I follow...

But can I take one step
without revealing my heart?
My whole life betrays me!

Even my silence is yours.

But it would be a lie to live any other way.

So I'll go on walking

(what else can I do?)

if you'll continue forgiving.

And I'll dare to see

where this strange life leads!

NOT TODAY

Today I won't look upon the waters;
I won't listen to songbirds
or smell fragrant flowers;
I won't feel the sun in my hands;
I'll hunger and thirst till tomorrow.
I'll be a body without senses.

IT'S NOT THE WAITING

It's not the waiting
  that causes suffering,
but the doubting
and the unknown.

A DREAM DEFERRED

Take me at my word:
This dream—undeterred,
relentless, unshaken;—
this desire deferred
will not be forsaken.

UNTIL THE HOUR

Don't tell me now,
but when the hour arrives,
what we will do when Time is ours
and all things are possible…
Tell me with your eyes!—
I want to believe in such incredible things!
But wait until the hour occurs;—
don't tell me now!

MAYBE I CAN RETURN

Maybe I can return
when I am lighter—
when the weight of the shadow dissipates.
And in the glow of that brief dawn,
will you welcome me?

I CAN STILL KNOW PEACE

I can still know peace

  despite this loss

if you tell me that it was only a battle

  and not the entire war.

THE AWAKENING

It was not planned: to be born in your eyes;
to have my monogram
woven into the fibers of your tapestry,
the warp to your weft,
hidden—never to be revealed
until the great unravelling of the threads.
No, it was not planned,
but a dream was awakened—
real or imaginary—
the moment I looked into your eyes.

DISTANT DREAMS

Portugal is sleeping, and I remain here—
drunk on its poetry,
desirous
to enter into its dreams;
to awaken at dawn
enwrapped
within its easygoing arms.

AFFINITY

Written on the face is truth,
revealing an affinity
that vibrates with sympathy.
We dance with words
carefully chosen,
peeling back layers
until the soul is reached.

IN YOUR GAZE

To love you or to let you go—
how shall I decide?
I'll know in a single glance
whether or not to stay:

If in pain you look my way,
I will turn from you;
but if with pleasure you gaze,
my burdens will flee.

VIRTUE

It throbbed in my veins, but I didn't feel;
it rang in my ears, but I didn't hear;
it stood before me, but I didn't notice...
because I only saw you.

NARCISSUS

What hand can harm you?

What man is your judge?

What wind directs your path?—

What woman will make you happy?

THE PATH OF DESIRE

The path of desire
is forged by aspiration
and followed with haste.

THE MADNESS OF LOVE

It swells within my breast:—
knowledge of Beauty.
But on these wings of madness,
of nothing am I certain!
Apart from water and sand,
who am I? and more,—from where?
If of spirit I was born,
I can love you well from afar.
But in this temporal body,
Patience and Passion
live together (but not as one)—
within the same heart.
And, with the same goal:—
to be near the Beloved.
Only one will achieve
the greater victory.

THE SWEETNESS OF THE FRUIT

To see but not to touch—
I would rather be blind!
To live but not to love—
for death I'd be ready!
To want, not to need—
the *sweetness* of the fruit!

STOICS

What stoics want with passion
is tempered with moderation.
But unless they are blind,
they are betrayed by their own eyes.

SUSPENDED

It's not the desire nor the fruit that is bad,
but the yielding—the tasting…
I don't want to live with the weight, so,
the sweetest fruit I've never tasted—
the desire within me—I know
still hangs on the tree…
still waits to be redeemed.

THE THORN

My reason, satisfaction;
on my flank, opposition.
My life, my pride;
my thorn in my side.

I CAN'T

I can't stand in the sun's path without burning;
I can't walk on these stones and not stumble;
I can't look upon deep waters without fear.
But I can't be withdrawn and isolated;—
I can't hide from the world if I want to live.

IGNIS FATUUS

Tell me I will never return—
that my hands will remain empty;
never more will I look upon the waters;—
that my hope was in vain,
my joy an illusion...
Tell me I will never return.

ENVY

"the value of others tortures us, revealing, with more clarity, our own nullity." — Teixeira de Pascoaes

The sun shines—I feel its warmth;
it shines for all, and I mourn not.
You glow in its light, and I sense your worth;
you shine for all—I weep in vain.

SOMETHING LIKE GRIEF

You know my desires;—

I've written them here, on these stones,

as if I were some god.

What is it, if not grief,

to feel robbed of something

that I had never possessed?

Is it then theft?

Then I am the thief!—

thief of my own imagination.

FAIN TO TASTE OF JOY

Fain to taste of joy,
yet this fruit wastes before me,
and from my mouth, flies.

A DREAM OF FOLLIES

Drawing breath from within shadows,—masks,
in a dream of nightmares and follies
that aligns itself with fragments from rafters
fallen from some funereal kingdom
where fear escapes from a hole,
from the earth;—from a grave of sadness
where no one distinguishes between night and day...

Giants dancing forth their glee
and sounding trumpets, brandishing glass...
fairies distancing themselves from merry mischief,
waiting attentively...
No one's ever suffered more than she.
No one's ever danced more than he
in this dream of nightmares and follies
where giants and fairies
draw breath from within shadows...

ANOTHER VISION

It burns in my memory: this dream that follows
a path different from that of my own two feet.
My verses reveal what the eyes do not see,
but the things of the world draw your eyes.
You saw neither me nor my heart;
you looked beyond and saw another vision.
I part ways with the morning and lean into the afternoon,
crossing the threshold of the terrace—and it burns...

THE FIRE THAT BURNS

Who says, "I want to see the sun
as it truly is"?
Many attributes, even when hidden,
are still recognized through faith.

(*If I am burned by its rays,*
I have only myself to blame.)
It's not like you—mysterious,
with layers to be unveiled;

with eyes that seek out weaknesses,
ready to tear down my defenses.
(*If they draw me in,*
who will save me?)

MY WAR

Every day the fire consumes.
Every day this war resumes,
and my wall weakens.
But I'll rise from the flames,
I'll reinforce my defenses,
I'll face a new day.
Not because I'm strong,
but because I love you.

SO HUMAN

I think upon the stones, eyes to the ground.
I obey not my own humble boundaries
learned from birth,
but those of some wayward soul
whose path is obscured by desire;
whose tears fall hot on the pavement—
burn hotter than the whitewash...

I think upon the waters with longing,
of deep sources where truth
is revealed in a daredevil gaze
in a clandestine garden dressed in white
where time stops and nothing is lost.
I dive in with reckless abandon.
So guilty, so innocent.

LINES WRITTEN ON AN AIRPLANE

“Sweet or salty?” she asked me.

“What is sweet?” I responded.

“Sweet is tradition and comfort;—

it satisfies, but it can make you fat.”

“And what is salty?”

“Salty comes like a wave

that swells and washes over you;—

you will be thirsty for more.”

I wanted them both,

but she said I could only choose one.

WINDS OF CHANGE

These ever-changing winds
leave me restless.
In the air is this uncertainty—
misplaced doubt.

But do you know that you are much more to me
than the thoughts
that pass by in the wind
tempting the senses?

Loving you is the beginning,
the middle, and the end.
It is the journey—and the way
back to you.

BOUNDARIES

It is blurred—the distinction
between what is yours and what is mine,
for I have imagined all that I know of you.
But from this Unknowing,
from out of some divine realm,
I have learned of love.

I don't prefer solitude,
but my heart is full
even though we cannot be together.
Yet I would reach out still,
at your first request,
if ever your arms became empty.

FORGIVENESS

They say forgiveness is divine—
an offering with no demands;
I'd like to think your flowers mine—
some gift of grace born from your hands.

AT THE DOOR

At the door of a lesser dream,
in the moment prior
to the point of capitulation,
grab my hand
and don't let me knock!

THE MEETING PLACE

This meeting place of spirits
in search of truth and illumination—
of dreams, reality, inspiration;
the silence in the music,
the calm before the storm…
This space between your eyes and mine
would render even the gods envious.

GARDEN OF SECRETS

Garden of secrets—
concealed paths
and murky waters
hide the truth.

Only a heart
free from deceit
lifts the veil
and reveals the light.

INTANGIBLE

If all that I have to offer you is nothing,
  will it be enough? In its essence,
it is priceless; but in its substance,
it has no value:
the fruit of my freedom:—
  my love.

LET IT BE LIKE THIS

If we should come to love each other,
let it be in freedom,
even with the freedom to leave.

And should we choose to leave,
let it be that we return—
that we return once more to one another.

But if love should die,
let it be at the same time;—
let it be at the same time, my love.

AUTONOMY

Love held tightly
seeks only to escape—
never to return.

Love held rightly
remains free
and always returns.

YOU SET ME FREE

You have released me.
Do you suppose I've now forgotten you?—
Never! For I was already free,
and I'll remember you always!

You had sincere thoughts;
you made the right decision,
but these arms will remain open
for this life is short!

Go and live your life
as if I never knew you;
and I will live mine
as though you are yet near!

SLOW TO PART

"Parting is such sweet sorrow"

I say goodbye with a divided will;
the best part of me loves you still.
Forgive me if I'm slow to part;
I'm waiting for your change of heart.

UNTIL THE HOUR (ANOTHER FAREWELL)

I want to reveal myself to you
(and you to me!)
like an open book that you read.
I want you to desire what you see—
to take me in your arms;
I want to take you in mine;
to drink deeply from the waters
that leave me thirsting for more.
We'll tremble like leaves,
we'll forget that we're mortal;
until the hour of your departure—
until the last page
is read...

I LINGER LONG

I linger long about your door,
and cast my shadow—nothing more.
These plaintive lines of poetry—
illusions of reality—
are writ in hopes to quench a fire
enkindled by my heart's desire...
My one desire, denied by fate,
that blooms inside the garden gate.
It seems my lot to wait and wait...

But Nature's true, and in due time,
the rose I sought to make but mine
will start to wither on the vine.
And fate proves kind, and in the end,
I'll come to see it as my friend;
for this I know with certainty:
all mingle with eternity...
One day I'll withdraw from your door,
and cast my shadow nevermore.

IF YOU TELL ME

If you tell me that this tree will never bear fruit,
I will stop watering it.
I will let it burn in the sun until it withers and dies.
But if you tell me that there is yet hope,
I will wait a lifetime
and keep it alive with my tears.

A MATTER OF SCIENCE

I don't need adulation from strangers—
 affirmation from algorithms
that promise to facilitate outcomes
 I've not even sought,—
that fulfill desires
 I never even dreamed of...
I only seek your presence
(it's not a matter of science);
I only desire your return;—
but not even *this* do I need!

NOW (TOSSED BY THE WAVES)

I let myself be tossed by the waves,
torn between there and here,
when the only *place* is *now*—
in this moment—where I've never been.

FREEDOM OF MOVEMENT

Freedom of movement
    forbidden by the body
quickens in the mind.

BEAUTIFUL PARADOX

We say goodbye
but never leave;
things change
yet stay the same.
My fever, my cure,—
beautiful paradox!
Together as one,
grow with me.

FROM DREAM TO DESTINY

Are you waiting to see me?
Then you will!
And you won't wait in vain.
Extend the hand;

we'll walk in dreams
among fields of rockrose.
I'll search your eyes—
dark like chestnuts,

and you will search mine—
gray as the sea,
reflected in yours,
lit by the moonlight...

We'll walk like this
from end to end of the dream,
waking at the last
to fulfill our destiny.

THE BEGINNING IN THE END

Give me your conclusion
and I'll return to the origin
of the question.

Give me your confusion
and I'll move in the direction
of clarity.

And as I search,
meaning and purpose
will begin to emerge.

Seeing the beginning in the end
gives me hope to carry on
and a reason to exist.

THE DIRECTION

At what time then, if not now?
And for what do you wait? What's the delay?
Fate is nothing but a false friend;
it brings only the promise of eternal sleep.
If you would be happy, follow only one thing:
the direction of your own choosing.

The Music in Your Words

...do not worry

if it is silence only

that reaches your ears:

it is music

still.

—Eugénio de Andrade

THE MUSIC IN YOUR WORDS

Listen for the music in your words;
it lies just beneath the doubt.
It enwraps the pain: a healing refrain—
a promise to return
whenever the tears fall.

Give it your all! Hold nothing back!
For this moment eternity waits.
Let it fall! let it rain!
till it returns anew to break through—
to penetrate the silence of the page.

WHAT A JOY!

What a joy it is to wield the pen—
unlike the tongue, which errs...
It brings such satisfaction,
this versification—
this hope that on a day more clear,
you will see yourself in my verses
and it will fill your heart.

SYNESTHETIC

Your soulful music fills the air.
Colliding droplets of sound
coalesce
and fall on my skin
like warm rain.
This is where we meet.

INSPIRATION

My reality is what I make of it;
so, what explains your presence?
I invent nothing about you, and yet,
there you are in the midst of my creation:
Beauty, clarity,—inspiration!

BEAT THE DRUM

from your heart
beat the drum
use both hands
hear me sing
lines of love

MAGIC SPELL

If there be cast a magic spell
upon this very heart,
'tis Beauty's craft—I know it well—
she makes of it an art.

MY MUSE

My muse is a place,
but it has a face, and a name,
and flies free as a dove.
My muse is Love.

A SOUL SUCH AS YOURS

You look upon the flowers
    and take in their beauty.
I look upon your face—
    more beautiful than they—
and know that my life
    is better for knowing
a soul such as yours
    who in beauty takes pleasure.

BEYOND REASON

Why do I love you?
Need I a reason?
You rise with the sun
and warm my heart!

So sacred, my dream—
to question it, treason.
How futile the answers
you search for in vain!

KINDRED

We are alike,
from the same source.
Pulse, water,
rhythm, life...

Dance with me until night;
remember me in your dreams.

THE OVERTURE

The softest music plays at the front.
In humble tones I make my plea;
but passion resounds in the background,
exposing a burning heart.

I give in to its overtures,
captured by the moment.
From the introductory chorus—
with its repetitive melodies—

to the final flourish,
I sing my desires.
I rest on a sweet note and search your eyes;—
but you give no sign.

THE WORDS

They sound so good in my head:
these words on the tip of my tongue—
words that wait for deliverance...

I speak but you say nothing.
I leave with your silence,
and my own words
ring in my ears...

Oh my solitude! Oh my heart!
I only wanted you to know,
I only wanted you to hear...

I'VE GIVEN YOU A NAME

Your dreams are my own
for I've given you a name
and that name is Love.

THE WORDS I LONG TO HEAR

What can I sing that has not been sung?
What can I write that has not been written?
Where else can I go when you are not with me?
Only you have the words that I long to hear.

I'LL SING OF LOVE

I will love you till I die;
until I die, I'll sing of love:
Love, which sees only beauty;
beauty, which beholds not death.

INDELIBLE

You left a poem on my cheek—
coarse, like wet sand
that clings to the skin.

I MEMORIZED YOUR FACE

I memorized your face
 like a conjugated verb—
  every aspect and mood.
Your name I whisper
like an oath—
  hidden in a Nocturne.

I RECALL YOUR WORDS

I recall your words

simply because they are few

and perspicacious.

THE SILENCE

Your name is written
on each page—
in every space
between words.
The last page—
the blank sheet—
it's yours too.

"WHEREVER YOU ARE"

"Wherever you are,
    wherever you are..."
The words ring in my ears
like church bells sounding forth promises,
sounding forth promises within the heart of me.

"Wherever you are,
    wherever you are..."
Can I believe in these words
even now that you're gone,
still finding comfort in you?

THE NEW ORPHEUS

You flee and I want to follow,
you sing and I want to soar;
because you are, I want to be.
But I can't tell you
if you don't look back,
and this you will not do.

ORPHEUS, STILL

You didn't need to look back,
but you looked back!
And now your gaze—
your gaze!—is all
that I see in this emptiness.
In my nothingness,
in my nothingness!—
My everything.

LYRA

I clung to hope, blindly,—
and, as if it was the last string
remaining on an ancient lyre, played it
carefully, methodically,
aware of the fragility, I played—
and strained to hear the single notes
vibrate against my heart in waves,
keeping it beating...
As the last string broke,
I feared for my heart. I removed my blindfold
and looked up in desperation;
I saw the stars keeping vigil;
I heard a song of Orpheus in the distance
and knew that I was not alone...

ON THE CENTENARY OF THE BIRTH OF EUGÉNIO DE ANDRADE (1923-2023)

Truth masked in verse
stands naked 'neath the veil—
unmoved by vain constructions.

SPIRIT SONG

What song today will you sing,
bird of my imagining?
With notes sublime that build, and build!—
tempt my heart and leave me thrilled!
For yesterday I was lost,
all alone and tempest-tossed,
and needed most your song to hear
caroled sweetly in my ear.
[We're much the same, you and I—
victims of the age-old lie
that the divine in us has fled—
left us lonely, left us dead.]
But you returned, as you do,
rendering my heart anew
with each new day, with some new song,
shepherding my life along!

SONG THRUSH

Songbird
always on the run
repeating sweet songs
and stealing my heart

MINGUS AT BAR DAS AVENCAS

Lines written upon hearing a Charles Mingus instrumental.

Slow and rhythmic,
a little melancholic:—
Music that says Goodbye,
more or less,
but entices you to stay—
recalling the sea...
Losing yourself
finding yourself
losing yourself...
Drifting in time,
or towards eternity...
Goodbye, more or less;
but more slow,
more rhythmic,—
less melancholic...

THE SONG OF THE THRUSH

When night is forgotten,
and Dawn appears,
I wait, I wait for the song of the thrush.

When the morning sun
brings the light that warms,
I hear, I hear the song of the thrush.

When shadows play
and the lime cools,
repeats, repeats the song of the thrush.

EVEN ROOSTERS HOLD THEIR BREATH

You play your music before the world,
but you hide your face when you sing.
Do you know that even roosters hold their breath
to listen while you call upon the dawn?

LULLABIES

I'll not keep you awake,
I'll sing you to rest;
for we remember best, since childhood,
the lullabies
more than the affairs of the day.

SWEET DREAMS

It awakens my senses—
the song of a bird.
It repeats—it repeats—
and brings joy to my ears!

So when I wish sweet dreams—
sweet dreams to my dear,—
I hope you'll find it a delight
to hear the same words every night.

THE ARMS THAT SAVE YOU

"Where do we quench this thirst for the infinite?"—Teixeira de Pascoaes

By refusing the one,
you accept the many,
and in turn, deny a truth.

In them you seek comfort,
but in turbulent seas,
the arms that save you bear the name *Saudade*.

REMEMBER THE FLOWERS

I could sue to the gods,
I could ask for a sign;
I could call you my love,
but you'd never be mine.

I could search for a key
that unlocks all the doors;
I could offer my heart,
but I'd never be yours.

So I'll write you a song
to remember the flowers,
and I'll sing of a love
that could never be ours.

A GENTLE WORD

Give me a gentle word,
for my heart is heavy
and I am without joy.
In my hand, ink beads
like sweat from the pen.
Even laughter brings grief,
and joy ends in sorrow.
Give me a gentle word.
Show me mercy!

RESURGENT

Poetry that falls on deaf ears
rises on wings
to more receptive skies.

NO ACCORD OF MAN

No accord of man
can keep a heart from loving—
caged birds from singing.

I FILL YOUR SILENCE

I fill your silence with music

yet hear you still

between each measure.

GREATNESS

To achieve a goal with ardor

is an admirable feat for a youth.

But to taste love in this life

is the greatest victory of a man.

DEARTH

Who envisions paradise
if not the imperfect?—
knows joy better
than those who suffer?
Creation springs
from lonely hearts;
with their longing,
they fill a void.

DISTINCTIONS

I'm not living in the past
if I write in the present, am I?
For putting feet to the path
is like a pen in the hand.

The distinction between the imaginary
and the real is created by me,
whether it be a solitary line
or verses filled with you.

TO ME, YOU ARE PORTUGAL

Forgive me these lines!
To me, you are Portugal—
how could I not sing?

PORTUGAL

This people, this land...
Oh! how beautiful you are!
Do you even know?
You are a treasure
hidden in my heart;
a source of inspiration,
an unwritable poem—
Portugal!

PORTUGAL, STILL

You are Portugal—still—
in my memory, my dreams.
In fullness of life,
in essence of being.

You are Portugal—still—
"that poet on the loose"*—
creator of beauty
with nothing to lose!

You are Portugal—still—
and I'll always remember
how the weight of these words
was received with delight.

*Agostinho da Silva

A PLACE OF JOY

I will write my words
from a place of joy
and not from a place of pain.
Even sadness can be sweet
when wrapped in love,
but bitter when isolated.

THERE WILL ALWAYS BE SUNSHINE

There will always be sunshine
and birds on the wing
And a place in my heart
that delights when they sing
There will always be moonlight
and stars within view
But right now there's just me
and me thinking of you

MY DESCANT

I offer neither gold
    nor hollow promises,
only the enduring dreams
    of girls and old women.

Less innocent now,
    less hesitant,
naked here before you,
    I sing my descant.

WILL YOU LISTEN?

Can you hear me still?
If you want to, you will...
The thought makes me smile,
and I think on it a while.
Maybe in a reverie,
or in the opening of a leaf,
you'll recognize the melody
and know that it's me.
Perhaps you will hear—
you will hear me, and smile!

STILL HAPPY

I awoke at dawn
and started singing
songs written for you.

I heard the birds outside;
it seemed as if
they were singing just for me.

And amidst our chorus
I began to smile,
for I was happy, even though I knew
you could not hear us.

YOU, LOVE (ORIGINAL VERSION)

You, who taught my soul to sing,—
you,—who I made Everything
and Nothing at the same time,
filled my days and made them rhyme.
You, who answered my desire,
found my voice; you set on fire
things that wither and decay—
things that last but for a day;
not to show their ugly side,
but that in such things abide
eternity; and lovely!—
lovely, too, that vasty sea
where I found Peace,—or it found me.
For it was you who led me there,
led my spirit—unaware
that you would leave quick as you came
when once I dared to speak your name, "Love"...
Such the lesson of the rose:—
Beauty comes and Beauty goes,
yet in its wake a sweet perfume
fills the space in my heart-room.

To Dwell in Love

I speak of the garden where there begins
a clear day of entwined lovers.

—Eugénio de Andrade

THE CATALPA

The *catalpa* blooms
in the Gardens of Parede—
a stranger, like me.

TO DWELL IN LOVE

To dwell in love is like this:—
We enter into love freely,
and arrive continually.
Love has no beginning or end.

I HAVE TO LOOK DOWN

I have to look down

to walk on these stones,

and it reminds me of my pain.

Still, I keep walking.

LOOSE CHANGE

It's cold in Parede
  but for this loose change that keeps
warm in my pocket.

THE GARDEN WALL

Facing the garden wall,
I whisper my name;
but too soft for an echo,
it's caught up with the breeze.

Facing the wall,
I speak my name;
but timid and weak,
it falls to the ground.

Facing the wall,
I cry my name.
The wall responds, "She's here!"
But the garden already knew..

HOSPITALITY

Set the tables
Open the doors
Prepare your heart

Welcome the guests
Fulfill the requests
Offer your hand

Tell the story
Wipe your brow
Sing a song

Say your goodbyes
Close the doors
Give in to solitude

THE FIRST LIGHT

I arrived with the pigeons
that landed on the terrace,
with the first light that entered
through the windowpane,
to meet your eyes.

IN HIS FACE

In his face, a trace
of Greek god—formidable,
arresting beauty.

ABOVE ALL

I prize the sand on which you lie,
the space that seagulls
occupy above your head;
but more than these,
I prize you most especially.

GREEN THINGS

Green things—
Green things grow

in your window
where there is always sunlight.

Lovely things
that in your hands blossom

near the window
overlooking the sea.

THE ART OF TOUCH

The rose knows not where it came from,
but it knows well who cares for it.
I know the hands, but not the art—
the touch—that transforms it.

DESIGNS

Every stroke of your pen
on the piece of paper
is like a signature—
unique, verifiable
as a fingerprint—
like the veins in these leaves:
meandering, complex.
An intricate design
that reveals itself
in your imagination.

MY DESIRE (A NOCTURNE)

I'll take the bitterness from your lips;
from where it drips, I will drink, and I'll feel
your weight upon my own shoulders,—
leaving you to sleep in peace.

IF POETRY IS LIFE

If poetry is life,
then the words that I write are only illusions
unless they are lived.

If an ideal exists,
then this life is worth living
until the words come true.

AT LOVE'S TABLE (THE INVITATION)

Love sets the table,
serves the wine and the bread.
Wisdom, on my right,
holds my hand.

Come, sit at my left,
my muse, my vision!
There is no room for sorrow
when you hold my heart.

THE INVITATION

Lift the veil,
for a moment only,
to spy under what sky
I lay my head.

Remove the veil,
and see that, despite the distance,
we still harvest the same fruit—
partake of the same bread.

Tear the veil!—
Reveal my heart!
Recline with me at my table;
share the same bed.

THE KISS

Near the door, I'll leave my key
hidden in a potted tree.
When you arrive, let yourself inside;
I'll greet you with an eager kiss.

KISSES

Come here to my arms
with your kisses—
so warm on my cheek,
my neck...
With your hair—like gentle waves
that slip
and play between my fingers...
Come here to my arms;—
cover me with kisses.

GENTLE, THE NIGHT

Masculine are the hands that toil;—
fingers that bleed and swell...
bleed and swell
daily.

Feminine is the hair—the tears—
that wipe away the blood...
wipe away the blood
and take away the pain.

Gentle is the night that heals
when toil wins rest...
wins perfect rest
in an embrace.

WHO SEES THE FUTURE?

Who sees the future?
But in this moment,
to spend it with you
is all that I want.

THE BEST LIFE

In my memory
are mushrooms
filled with rainwater,
landscapes from travels
journeyed on foot,
verses laid down
in hopes
that I am still
in your good graces...

And at the heart
of my poems
lies a belief
so dear:
that to fill
all my days
with your presence
would be to live
the best life.

SOLITUDE (THE CRY OF A DOVE)

Never question my loyalty,
but never doubt my love;
because the cry of a dove
is only for her mate.

EVEN THESE STONES

Portugal! I love everything about you!—
even these stones that make me stumble...
Perhaps they are what I love the most.

RECOMPENSE

To entertain a thought so strange:
that I can never walk in this garden again.
It is a sad predicament, to be like this:
where my love has been my investment,
and my tears will be my reward.

DON'T LOOK BACK

Don't look back, they say,
never look back; but what if,
what if you look back?

ECHOES OF AN EMBRACE

Like it or not,
I accept this season
in which I find myself;
and I receive it, willingly,
with the memory
of the warmth of your embrace.

A BENEDICTION

May your memory be filled
with more smiles than tears,
more light than darkness,
more love than hate,
and more hope than despair.

MY PURPLE ROCK ROSE

You were born with a sensitive spirit,
with an ethereal essence.
You bloom every dawn—
my purple rock rose.

The world would be a better place
if it saw through your eyes.
Ray of sunshine, beautiful flower—
my purple rock rose.

When you were born, oh resilient bloom!—
kissed by the sun and the soil—
you filled my heart with love,
my purple rock rose.

A BLESSING

May the night be tender.
May it enfold you
the way I would hold you in my arms.

Before the Hand

...to see has always been to touch. To touch each thing, one by one, with the eyes, before the hand draws near...

—Eugénio de Andrade

BEFORE THE HAND

Before the hand that forms it,
before the eye that sees it—
inspiration.

It moves below the head,
the chest, the waist, the feet—
creation.

You show me my condition
with the ebbing of the tides—
revelation.

You bring the dawn—new life;
merciful you are—
restoration!

THE AUTHOR KNOWS

Nature plays her sweet songs,
  and I need not wonder for whom they're meant—
they're meant for me.
Because the author knows—
    the author knows
        the author knows
the rhythm of my heart.
It was his creation,
and it beats only because of him.
    It beats only for him
        beats only for him...

SINGULARITY

Within Nothingness exists an echo of Presence—
Force without form, Being without license.
A whisper of a voice well-loved,
reflected deep within my soul.

THE SPARK

Imagination is the remnant
of a dream of silence,
kindled where free will
meets destiny;
a spark—revealed
within reality
and refined by truth—
that transforms
and gives meaning to existence.

I BREATHE

My breath comes from God,
but it was you whom I breathed
into these verses.

AS THE DEER

"He who sows the wind reaps the whirlwind."

I drink it deeply:
this hot cup of bitterness,
oppressive in its thickness,
offensive to the tongue.
Oh, my spirit rises up like acid—
take it from my lips!
If it be within your power,
let me abide in your grace,
to pant, like the deer,
for living water.

THE ESTUARY (A LITANY)

"'There is no death... There is no death... / No death...'" —Joseph Courtney, Lieut., R.A.M.C., in "As the Leaves Fall" (Autumn, 1916)

Standing by the water's edge,
gold against a leaden sky,
rooted firm by reed and sedge,
echoing the warbler's cry—
in communion, he and I.

To defy the coming cold,
spider weaves his finest thread.
Here, no thought of growing old
rises from the riverbed.
I lie down and rest my head.

Blanketed by morning mist,
murmurs fill my reverie:
Hoverflies, sea aster-kissed,
speak to me like poetry—
every line in harmony.

On the branch and on the stem,
what is left of leaf and flower
graze against my garment's hem,
offering their healing power—
sages of the reedy bower.

Startled by a foe revealed,
migratory birds break ranks,
scatter to a distant field
farther down the river's banks.
Solemnly, I offer thanks:

For the sky and for the sedge,
for the reeds by water's edge;
for the spider weaving thread,
for the pillow 'neath my head;
for these lines of poetry,
for the hope of harmony;
for the healing from the flower,
for my company this hour;
for the gift of life, of breath—
for the God who conquered death.

KEEP ME STEADY

Keep me steady, for I fear the wind
and where it may blow.
But it's you, Lord, who dictates its course,
who stills the waves into repose.
What storm can unsettle you?

LABYRINTH

It's a puzzle to me, a labyrinth...
and I would be lost
trying to keep up with
all the twists and turns
if not for the fact
that my compass
is already oriented
toward True North.

WITH WHAT REMAINS

You have already judged me.
There is nothing more that I can say.
The me that I see mirrored in your eyes
I can't even recognize.
Too deep for words,
and impossible to tell,
I've walked this road a long time
and the subtleties are hard to remember.
With what is left of life to live,
with what is left of me to save,
I will carry to the heavens
to give unto my God.

THE BATTLE

He said that the battle
was his and not mine.
But what does he desire?
That I fight in his strength,
or lay down my sword?

BATTLE-RHYTHM

"yet somewhere there is God." —William Dean Howells

There is only noise
 where rhythm is lacking;
discordant sounds—
the din of war.

Or else there is silence
where rhythm is lacking;
a profound hush—
death in battle.

But a God of harmony
turns cries into song;
and in the face of war,
even the fallen sing.

24 FEBRUARY 2022

Vain delusion wields the knife,
"oneness" is his battle call
justifying war and strife—
rhetoric before a fall.

(Tyranny, he comes too late!
Peace already sealed his fate.)

Freedom that his lips belie—
sanctioning enslavement still—
Will you not his words decry?
Will you war against your will?

(Tyranny, you come too late—
Peace already sealed your fate!)

ONLY TO LOVE

Animals fix their sight on the throat
 when they go in for the kill.
But what primordial instinct do we follow?—
 to advance, but not for ill...
And the hands—if not to tear and claw—
 what natural code do we obey?
What instinct? What law? Only that of a King
 who commands of our will...
  but to love!

THE WINDSTORM

How can I withstand this windstorm
and not be swept away?
I've no roots strong enough
to keep me grounded...
So I will fly,
and I will trust,
and I'll be moved,
and I'll be safe,
because the Source of this wind
directs its path.

BURDENS

My burden is heavy,
    can you bear it?
My doubts are many,
    can you relieve them?
You hold my heart
    and keep it beating;
I'm safe in your hands
    for you give me strength to live...
Your burden is light, I will accept it.
You give me rest;—I trust in you.

FORBIDDEN, FORGIVEN

If not forbidden,
would the fruit still seem
so beautiful on the tree?

If not forgiven,
could the tongue forgo
the sweetness of the flesh?

PRAGMATIC POEM (IRREVOCABLE)

No good offering, once given,
can be lost—
nor be taken from the giver.
No falsehood negates the gift.
The reality of a life well-lived
cannot be altered
by any narrative created
with the intent to change history,
but resides eternally in Memory,
one day to be revealed.

PRAGMATIC POEM (DISCRETION)

To tell all your dreams bears a risk;
why not leave elements to mystery?
Discretion is employed by the wise;
so, temper what falls from your lips.

PRAGMATIC POEM (DOUBT)

It may seem illogical,
but doubt itself can sustain
the heart that questions and waits…

One aspect of being human
is the ability to accept
that there is possibility in uncertainty—

to search for meaning in the absurd…
What we don't know, we can believe
and make it so.

PRAGMATIC POEM (THE OBJECT OF MY LOVE)

It may appear that I only live
for the object of my love.
I do not. I live to love,
and the object fulfills the objective.

AN EASTER LAMENT

You have overcome death.
Help me overcome my tears;
help me to overcome myself,—
because I'm not even trying,
I'm not even trying...

LAZARUS

With me, Lazarus,
be patient, be forgiving;
for you were as dead,
and I was lost.
Help me to believe again,
oh my brother, in you, in myself,—
in the heart!

THE OLD BARK

Carry the old bark out to sea.
With the pitying tides, let him drift.
Take him to where the Captain dwells;
resigned, calm, free—he will sail.

RENEWAL

What, then, is death
if not the condition
imposed upon both the weak and the strong
that brings forth renewal?

We know beauty
as the fruit of our pain.
So it is in nature:
From ashes comes the flower!

Such decay
gives rise to new life.
But how can righteousness
spring from our guilt?

It can only be atoned for
by one who is blameless.
It comes from God—
a gift freely given.

PER ASPERA

I was made not only to breathe,
but through this suffering,
to reach the starry sky.
This is what the worlds hope for.

IN THE SEED

Because I lacked faith,
I gave myself to my passion
which rots like ripe fruit
after it falls to the ground.

But in the seed—the remains of the fruit—
there is already room for growth,
for nature saves it from the dust
and gives it new birth.

FROM GOOD SEED

Why cry? why now?
when everything is in its place,
and as it should be.
What can be said?—
From good seed grows the flower,
and from that flower, the fruit.
Why then the grief?
And what has changed about the sea?
Not one thing!
It heals the body and restores the soul.
This is its office.
You say it's Nature that you love?
Work the soil! Bear good fruit!
Be baptized in the waters!
And all tears will dry,
and you will find Peace!

MERCY

We carry sorrows on our backs like burdens,
but they should fall off like old leaves from an olive tree.
We swim in the waters to lighten the weight,
and find that they are washed away by Mercy.

NONE OTHER

No body of water bears my name;
to no noble crown do I lay claim.
Yet let not my lips malign or defame,
and suffer my critics to do the same.

For no other being shares my shame,
and no other god assumes my blame
but He whose love for me became
my Comforter and Living Flame.

COMMUNION

Full of joy,
despite their pains,
like butterflies to flowers,
they approached the fount
and shared the elements
of remembrance.

Weighing the heart,
they broke bread and ate;
they took the cup and drank,
meditating on the sacrifice
and receiving the blessing
of communion.

THE GOD IN YOU

To live in us forever,
He had to leave us;
but he promised to come back again—
our souls to comfort.

He said it would be like this:
Where he is, we are.
If he is present in us,
we will never be apart.

The God in you is the God in me;—
we don't have to say goodbye.

TRY YOUR HAND AT LOVE

To try our hand at love is not to waste
one single moment, nor to breathe our last;
we reconcile the present with the past,
believing in a joy in which we've placed

our greatest hope. Yet, in our side, a thorn
reminds us that in weakness and in pride,
it's not in earthly things that we abide,
but in the One in whom we are reborn.

To try our hand at love is more to meet
a shadow of the divine and the pure—
surrendering to all that we endure—
to lay to rest our cares at someone's feet.

To try our hand at love is to know God:
To rise as if to Heaven from the sod.

THE NARROW GATE

I know that the gate is narrow;
I've seen it, and my heart desires.
I know that this life is short,
but the way seems so long

and I'm already weary.

TESTIMONY

In freedom, build unambiguous monuments,
so that in times of oppression,
when these symbols are torn down,
all will bear witness to the transgression.

And what of Peace? Without justice, peace is bankrupt;
even dictators sing its song...
Let *Freedom* be on your tongue,
and the cry of your heart!

SIGNS

I don't trust in signs.
I trust that I'll be led,
that I will be fed
by the Giver, through His Gift.
Nor will I speak of signs.
I'll speak only of His Name;
for signs can deceive,
and there is no one more trustworthy
upon whom I may call.

BEAUTY'S TRIBUTE

Lovingly I gaze, longingly I weep
  over your landscape, watering these stones.
How distant are the lands, and vast the sea
  that lies between, and I ache in my bones...
But a poet* once mused that though man lauds
  from afar, still must he yearn for beauty—
though his passion be dumb. Praise be to God,
  who provides peace and hope in sympathy;
who grants us to grieve, but never alone,
  and only for a time... But as I stand,
my time seems borrowed, my peace all but
    flown.
  Yet only fools obey what fear commands,
and your beauty I seek! So seek I will—
passionless if I must—to laud you still!

*Florence Earle Coates

STILL LIFE

What happens in my mind
affects my body;
If I say that I am dying,
then I'm already dead.
Be still and silent,
oh my soul;
Know the peace that mercy brings
and encounter life!

STILL, I LIVE

In your eyes, I've already lived;

and yet,

I'm still living.

You poured out your grace

over my weakness

before I was born,

yet it remains

as fresh to me

as each new dawn.

WE'LL SEE

We'll see, we'll see...
Life is good,
I can't complain.

God provides, God provides.
In His hands
I will abide.

I love, I love
this garden,
this land.

I'll remember, I'll remember
waters that inspire,
sunlight that heals,
birds that sing...

THE JOURNEY

Over palaces and villages,
the sea and the hills,
over all the good earth, we will soar.

Without knowing where we're going,
like the wind among the branches,
we'll be free—accepting all the risks.

And as we look back,
we'll understand that the peace
that journeyed with us had been God.

THE UNIVERSAL LIGHTHOUSE (A NOCTURNE)

Fog that obscures the sunset
and the purple nocturnal sky
cannot hide the universal

lighthouse that burns in my chest.
My will keeps it burning;
for this end I was made:

Never to extinguish, always to be
singular of purpose:
a candle to receive

the solitary traveler.

WIND AND SPIRIT

The wind is neither seen nor heard
until it moves things.
Until it whispers through the leaves;—
until the trunks bend
    and sway
        and knock...
Until the waters dance upon the surface,
    move my soul,
        and fill me with joy.

WINESKINS

He pours out new wine
into these skins already
portending ruin.

NOCTURNE (COUNTER-MELODY)

Heaven exists

Heaven exists

or I'll never

see you again

Heaven exists

Heaven exists

or I'll never

see you again

Oh I'll see you

I'll see you

I'll see you

again

I'll see you

I'll see you

I'll see you

again

ENVOI

If it be not you

who waits for me at the door,

let it be Mercy!

Tudo Passa

But how can one make this mouth, this sun,
last until the final instant?

—Eugénio de Andrade

PERFECT TIME

Everything in Nature moves in perfect time,
although some things seem to move with haste:—
The fury of the wind during a storm;
a startled bird taking flight;
waves that break against the shore;
the morning light,
and the beating of my heart.

FLIES AND FALLS

Time flies, night falls. It flies and falls
from day to night, from green to white,
the seasons of her being.
Prepared is she for each new dawn,
come what may.

She flies, she falls. She flies and falls,
ever landing in the sympathetic embrace
of a fading memory.
Here she is content,
and here remains.

TUDO PASSA

Upon my spirit the days press
with confident hands, yet lightly.
Joy and grief they know not;
only that all things pass and return again.

HOW BRIEF THE HOUR

Oh, Dawn!—
how brief is the hour
that ushers in the day.

ASYNCHRONY

As the sun decays
over Cascais like a flame,
it burns still for me.

NOW

Whether I'm facing the sun
or looking back at my shadow,
I'm still exactly where I am,
and you're exactly where you are.

WHAT IF?

What if I were like the wind?—
sometimes kind, sometimes harsh;
restless and unpredictable.

What if I were like the sea?—
ever-changing, mysterious;
vast and unfathomable.

But I'm just like me—
nothing more, nothing less;
a being, complete and incomparable.

THE HEAT OF SUMMER

In the heat of summer,
 when sweat is on the brow,
a fond look
brings the shade of the forest.

YOU ARE

You're the "easy" in "take it easy"—
the bridge of a song;
flowers in springtime—
cool waters in summer.

And when I find myself
adrift in the tides,
I remember these comforts—
reminders of who you are.

YOU DRIVE ME WILD

Each morning, my whole body wakes.
    You are far from me,
but the trees bear fruit;—it is late Spring
and I think of you; you drive me wild.

As light lingers overhead,
    it warms my limbs.
I think of your touch—of how it will be
when I see you again;—you drive me wild.

You may ask what I'm thinking
    when day is done:
How I feel, if life is good…
But darling, you know!—you drive me wild!

AT MY SIDE

They caress your skin: the waves.

"I love you, I love you, I love you…" they say.

In the sand, I bury my feet—

a wistful observer.

The same sun that heals your ills

fills my head with fever.

But Mercy is at my side;

I close my eyes and sigh.

A DREAM UNTASTED

A dream untasted
is sleep wasted.

IMAGINATION

I don’t await the light, though it is night.
I close my eyes, and with my mind,
create sparks that illuminate the dark,
eliminate my fear, and dream
as if it were already here.

SPLASHES OF PAINT

1.—DREAMS

I navigate the narrow streets in the dark,
interpreting my dreams.
They come to me in somber gray…
I offer them my solemnity
and paint them with positivity.

SPLASHES OF PAINT

2.—REFRACTION

Sunlight travels the long path
through the atmosphere and paints the sky
in yellow, orange, and red.

SPLASHES OF PAINT

3.—SWELLS

They rise and fall,
wave upon wave:
Ribbons of gray
in unbreaking undulations
driven
by distant storms.

OH NATURE!

Oh Nature! I had forgotten you—
not the imitation, but the True!
Where a weary soul can find rest
when even Art is politicized.

CHANGES

The wind brings changes
despite our will;
it blows kisses to chidren,
and to grown-ups, longing.

HOPE, MY JOY

With every breath
that lacked joy,
I gathered memories
like wildflowers,
and formed a wreath
to adorn my head.

HOPE IS THE SAPLING

Hope is the sapling
 that grows within the hollow
of a dying tree.

IF I KNEW

I don't know what makes the days long,

but I'd give you the peace of heaven

if I could.

Nor do I know what dries the tears,

but I'd share the secret—

if I knew.

A GOOD HARVEST

Fruits form quickly.
It is the ripening
that tests our will
while we wait, preparing
for a good harvest
never promised to us.

SATISFACTION

The mouth of a baby
summons the fingers,
and she is soothed.
As long as we live,
it's still the mouth
that seeks satisfaction;—
still the hand that obeys,—
bringing the fruit
that ripens
with time.

THE FIRES

In the fields, the fires burn.
Would that these tears
could extinguish the flames,
but they reach them not;
nor do they return inward,
where, in my chest, they also burn.

The fires burn in the fields,
yet I spy green among the ashes;
there is life beneath the soil
that awaits the rain.
And somewhere out there is a hand
to dry my eyes.

LIKE A FLOWER

Like a flower—
Petals open to the world at morn,
and folded without regret at day's end.
Without regret,
without lament—
like a flower.

SUMMER WIND

There's a summer wind
In the fall
Maybe it's a sign
So I dream

There's a summer wind
In the fall
But I know what time it is
I'm no fool

There's a summer wind
In the fall
I put on my windbreaker
And I cry

FAITHFUL AUTUMN

Doubtful the harvest,
but Autumn has come despite
and sets the world right.

AUTUMN BREEZE

I knew you as the autumn breeze
when, in my youth, I blithely walked
along raked paths of fallen leaves;—
I knew you as the autumn breeze.

The birds that died, I buried there
along raked paths of fallen leaves;
without a thought, without a care,
the birds that died, I buried there.

Within the branches high above,
without a thought, without a care,
the songbirds sang of my first love
within the branches high above.

* * *

And even now, midst fallen leaves,
as gently blows the autumn breeze,
without a thought, without a care,
the birds that die I bury there.
And in the branches high above,
still sing the birds of my first love.

ONE COLD MORNING

The pond is still this morning.
Onto a thin layer of ice,
a tear falls and freezes.
The fish are oblivious to the cold.

BEFORE THE DAWN

Impatient blossom, hear my song!—
I know the winter lasted long,
yet he wins faith who trusts in Time,
who, far removed from warmer climes,
would heed this counsel that I bring
and overwinter till the Spring.
For naught but wormwood has the seed
that disregards such crucial need.
And early here and early gone
who, restive, rise before the dawn.

CHILDHOOD DREAMS

They were timeless,
 the days that I became a child again.
But as I write these lines,
I seem only aware of the time.
And yet, I forget not my dreams,
for the dreams of a child are pure,
and fill my days with hope.

WE AGE

We age,
but our shadow stays young.
It pulls on us like a child
eager to tell a secret.
But we stop listening,
and so we age.

THE LONG-AWAITED NIGHT

This day is long, but forgiving;
for I know that it brings
the long-awaited night
in which labors cease;—
when mind and hands
are occupied
with joys that satisfy
and bring peace.

BRING THE DARKNESS

Bring the darkness,
but let me rest;
give me solitude,
but let me have peace.
But return to me on sad days
and be my light.

PEACE

I do not desire peace that comes
only when the sun is bright,
but peace that comes as a gift
during a storm.

THE GOAL OF VICTORY

If your gain is my loss,

then what a sweet loss it is!

Your sky brightens;—

mine darkens.

But never before was there

such sweet darkness,

nor have the stars ever shone so

intensely!

LEGACY

As the seasons pass,
may they say, "She loved."
Let that be the truth;
let these leaves speak of her.

INDEX OF TITLES

A

B

C

D

E

F

INDEX OF TITLES

INDEX OF FIRST LINES

INDEX OF FIRST LINES

INDEX OF FIRST LINES

INDEX OF FIRST LINES

INDEX OF FIRST LINES

INDEX OF FIRST LINES

INDEX OF FIRST LINES

About the Book

In a Language Not Your Own is a collection of Portugal-inspired English-language poems by Sonja N. Bohm, shaped by an encounter with the Lisbon landscape and drawn from bilingual work composed simultaneously in English and Portuguese during the author's introduction to the Portuguese language.

Acknowledgments

My gratitude to the poetry of Eugénio de Andrade and Teixeira de Pascoaes, whose writings accompanied me while learning Portuguese; and to Florence Earle Coates, who taught me that "truth is with the dreamer." Her words are to me as daily bread, and her voice quietly shaped the listening and attentiveness that made this book possible.

Pas
coaes
OS COBREM
RAMOS NOS
DAS A
ÁRVORES TODOS

www.ingramcontent.com/pod-product-compliance
Lightning Source LLC
LaVergne TN
LVHW010645110826
845149LV00014B/2965
9798999570925